Good News, Bad News

News Stories for Listening and Discussion

Roger Barnard

NATIONAL UNIVERSITY
American Language and Intercultural Studies
(619) 563-2657

Oxford University Press

Oxford University Press

198 Madison Avenue, New York, NY 10016 USA
Great Clarendon Street, Oxford OX2 6DP England

Oxford   New York
Athens   Auckland   Bangkok   Bogotá   Bombay
Buenos Aires   Calcutta   Cape Town   Dar es Salaam
Delhi   Florence   Hong Kong   Istanbul   Karachi
Kuala Lumpur   Madras   Madrid   Melbourne
Mexico City   Nairobi   Paris   Singapore
Taipei   Tokyo   Toronto

and associated companies in
Berlin   Ibadan

OXFORD is a trademark of Oxford University Press.

ISBN 0-19-434873-3

Copyright © 1998 Oxford University Press

Library of Congress Cataloging-in-Publication Data
Barnard, Roger.
   Good news, bad news : news stories for listening and
discussion / Roger Barnard.
     p. cm.
   ISBN 0-19-434873-3
   1. English language--Textbooks for foreign speakers.
2. Listening--Problems, exercises, etc. 3. Discussion--
Problems, exercises, etc. I. Title.
PE1128.B3216   1997
   428.3′4--dc21
                    97-9465
                    CIP

No unauthorized photocopying.

All rights reserved. No part of this publication may be
reproduced, stored in a retrieval system, or transmitted,
in any form or by any means, electronic, mechanical,
photocopying, recording, or otherwise, without the
prior written permission of Oxford University Press.

This book is sold subject to the condition that it shall
not, by way of trade or otherwise, be lent, resold, hired
out, or otherwise circulated without the publisher's
prior consent in any form of binding or cover other
than that in which it is published and without a similar
condition being imposed on the subsequent purchaser.

Editorial Manager: Chris Foley
Project Manager: Paul Riley
Developmental Editors: Ellen Kisslinger, Bev Curran
Contributing Editor: Karen Brock
Production Editor: Anita Raducanu
Designer: Mark Kellogg
Picture Researcher: Clare Maxwell
Production Manager: Abram Hall
Production Services: A Plus Publishing Services

Printing (last digit): 10 9 8 7 6 5 4 3 2 1

Printed in Hong Kong.

ACKNOWLEDGMENTS
Illustrations by Randy Verougstraete
Radio icon and illustration on p. 30 by Eliot Bergman
Cover design by Mark Kellogg
Cover illustration by Rob Schuster

The publisher would like to thank the following for their
permission to reproduce texts:
Stories 1, 2, 6, 7, 9, 10, 13, 15, 16, 17: © Associated Press.
   Reprinted with permission.
Stories 3, 5, 8: © Reuters. Reprinted with permission.
Story 4: © Asahi Press. Reprinted with permission.
Story 11: © UPI. Reprinted with permission.
Stories 12, 14, 18: © AFP/Jiji. Reprinted with permission.
p. 36: CALVIN AND HOBBES © Watterson. Dist. by
   UNIVERSAL PRESS SYNDICATE. Reprinted with
   permission. All rights reserved.
p. 46: Record for the Longest Wait for a Sale: World
   copyright © Guinness Publishing Ltd 1986
p. 48: Records from the Guinness Book of Records 1997
   World copyright © Guinness Publishing Ltd 1996

The publisher would like to thank the following for their
permission to reproduce photographs:
p. 12: © John G. Ross/Photo Researchers, Inc.
p. 39: Dr. Seth Shostak, Science Photo Library/Photo
   Researchers. Inc.
p. 51: © Michael A. Keller, Studio Ltd./The Stock Market

The author and publisher would like to thank the following
reviewers for their valuable comments and suggestions:

Eleanor Barnes   Terry O'Brien
David Clay Dycus   Jack Perkins
David Dykes   Carol Rinnert
Marion Friebus   Tina Rowe
Robert Hickling   Peggy Rule
Keith Lane   Scott Rule
Paul Lewis   Oscar Ulloa
Mary Sisk Noguchi Junko Yamanaka

CONTENTS

STORY 1: Dream Jackpot   1

LISTENING FOR GIST	LISTENING FOR INFORMATION	LISTENING FOR DETAILS	SPEAKING	USEFUL LANGUAGE
Choosing the best question	Following a sequence: ordering pictures	Identifying information in context	Discussion: *Dreams*	*Have you ever had a dream about...?*

STORY 2: False Alarm   4

LISTENING FOR GIST	LISTENING FOR INFORMATION	LISTENING FOR DETAILS	SPEAKING	USEFUL LANGUAGE
Choosing the best headline	Following a sequence: ordering sentences	Understanding questions and identifying the correct response	Preferences survey: *Flying*	*Which do you prefer...?*

STORY 3: A Fishy Story   7

LISTENING FOR GIST	LISTENING FOR INFORMATION	LISTENING FOR DETAILS	SPEAKING	USEFUL LANGUAGE
Identifying the best summary	Following a sequence: ordering pictures	Identifying factual details	Story telling and fact checking: *Losing things*	*"Wh"* questions

STORY 4: A Long Trip   10

LISTENING FOR GIST	LISTENING FOR INFORMATION	LISTENING FOR DETAILS	SPEAKING	USEFUL LANGUAGE
Choosing the best question	Distinguishing factual information: *True* or *False*	Using numbers in context	Making plans: *Travel*	• *First/Then/Next/After that* • *"Wh"* questions

STORY 5: Having a Ball   13

LISTENING FOR GIST	LISTENING FOR INFORMATION	LISTENING FOR DETAILS	SPEAKING	USEFUL LANGUAGE
Choosing the best headline	Following a sequence: ordering sentences	Identifying numerical details	Making plans: *Dream dwelling*	Using *"would"* to discuss hypothetical situations

STORY 6: Sea Mail   16

LISTENING FOR GIST	LISTENING FOR INFORMATION	LISTENING FOR DETAILS	SPEAKING	USEFUL LANGUAGE
Choosing the best response to a question	Distinguishing factual information: *True* or *False*	Understanding questions and identifying the correct response	Pair work activity: *Message in a bottle*	*Which message is the most...?*

STORY 7: Easy Come, Easy Go   19

LISTENING FOR GIST	LISTENING FOR INFORMATION	LISTENING FOR DETAILS	SPEAKING	USEFUL LANGUAGE
Identifying the best summary	Following a sequence: ordering pictures	Identifying factual details	Group activity: *Shopping spree*	Using *"would"* to discuss preferences

STORY 8: Best Commuter   22

LISTENING FOR GIST	LISTENING FOR INFORMATION	LISTENING FOR DETAILS	SPEAKING	USEFUL LANGUAGE
Choosing the best question	Distinguishing factual information: *True* or *False*	Understanding questions and producing an appropriate response	Survey and discussion: *Commuting*	• *How do...?* • *How long does...?* • *What do...?*

STORY 9: A Drop-out   25

LISTENING FOR GIST	LISTENING FOR INFORMATION	LISTENING FOR DETAILS	SPEAKING	USEFUL LANGUAGE
Choosing the best headline	Following a sequence: ordering sentences	Understanding questions and identifying the correct response	Role-play activity: *Interviewing someone*	*Can I ask you a few questions...?*

INTRODUCTION

Good News, Bad News was written out of a desire to help students take advantage of the proliferation of English-language international news broadcasts in recent years. While radio and satellite television broadcasts are available worldwide, the difficulty of understanding the language used by the media makes them inaccessible to many learners.

Good News, Bad News is a course designed to help pre-intermediate and intermediate students improve their general listening and speaking abilities while focusing on the skills needed to understand broadcast news. It features a collection of entertaining stories based on news taken from actual wire service reports. Each three-page unit focuses on a story presented in radio news format. By teaching students to recognize and exploit the organization of typical news stories, *Good News, Bad News* prepares them to understand real news broadcasts.

Each unit features a sequence of task-based activities that lead students from general to detailed understanding of the story. First, students are given a structured task that requires them to listen for the main point, or gist, of the news report. In the next two listening activities, they "zoom in" on the important or interesting details. Afterwards, they discuss the content or theme of the news story in a structured speaking activity. An optional **Extra Practice** section in the back of the book provides students an opportunity to complete a modified cloze activity by filling in missing words in the tapescript.

The listening activities in *Good News, Bad News* are primarily receptive tasks. This means students engage in activities such as matching items in columns, answering multiple choice or true/false questions, or ordering pictures in a sequence to show they have understood what they heard. A minimal amount of language production is necessary. The rationale behind this is the following: When students listen to something, they must use another skill, such as speaking or writing, to express what they have understood. If a student cannot say or write the correct answer, this does not necessarily mean the student did not understand the information. It may only mean the

student does not have strong speaking or writing skills.

Although the emphasis of *Good News, Bad News* is on developing listening skills, there are ample opportunities for speaking practice in each unit. Once students complete the structured listening tasks, they are encouraged to engage in a variety of expansion activities that promote speaking and provide opportunities to improve their conversational competency.

Course Components

A **Student Book,** comprised of 18 Units and an Extra Practice section at the back of the book.

An **Audio Program** of the news stories available on **cassette** and **compact disc,** featuring American, British, Australian, and Asian newsreaders.

A **Teacher's Book,** that contains:
- step-by-step instructions for each unit
- optional speaking activities
- photocopiable resource pages
- cultural and language notes
- photocopiable tapescripts with content notes
- answer keys

Student Book Organization

The stories in *Good News, Bad News* have been sequenced to balance serious and less serious topics. Each unit is self-contained, and the level of difficulty in terms of vocabulary and structures remains relatively constant throughout the course; this means the stories can be taught in any order.

Each unit contains the following sections:

▶ Tuning In

Exercise 1 is primarily a schema-building activity. In other words, students are asked to make observations about the illustration that introduces the story and predict what happens in the story. They discuss general questions that stimulate interest in the topic, as well as activate their vocabulary and background knowledge.

Exercise 2 is a vocabulary-building activity that identifies and teaches new language contained in the news story. Fill-in-the blank, matching, and sentence completion exercises are used. Students are encouraged to work together to share what they already know.

▶ Good News, Bad News

Exercise 1 asks students to listen for the main idea of the story. They identify the best headline, a one-line summary, or the best question or answer in a conversational exchange. The primary goal at this stage is general understanding.

Exercise 2 gives students the opportunity to listen to the story again and asks them to identify the important points of the story. This exercise may be in the form of a true/false activity, ordering pictures, or ordering sentences based on the story. Again, listening for every word is discouraged.

Exercise 3 focuses on additional factual details of the story. Exercise types include multiple-choice, fill-in-the-blanks, and in later units, supplying short answers in an interview. Some of the items include sound discriminations, particularly with numbers.

▶ Signing Off

This is a communicative speaking activity that builds on the theme of the story and provides opportunities for student personalization. Students work in pairs or small groups to exchange ideas and information through a variety of tasks, such as surveys, discussions, and role plays.

▶ Extra Practice

This is a modified cloze activity that presents the tapescript of each story with 12 words or phrases missing. The deletions include the six items in the **Tuning In 2** section, plus six items selected to promote vocabulary development. This is an optional consolidation activity, and can be used before or after **Signing Off**. Students will benefit most by turning to the **Extra Practice** section only after completing the other listening activities in the unit.

Flexibility

The complete unit is designed to take 60–90 minutes of class time. The amount of time devoted to a particular section will depend on the main purpose for choosing the book: listening or speaking. For a listening course, you may decide to skip the **Signing Off** activities. However, for a conversation class, less time may be spent on the listening activities, and the news story may be used as the foundation for a variety of speaking tasks. The **Teacher's Book** provides expansion activities for each unit. These activities can be adapted to multi-level classes.

Photocopiable Teacher Resource Pages

The **Teacher's Book** includes photocopiable activity and assessment pages, along with photocopiable tapescripts. The activity sheets, particularly suitable for use with expansion activities outside of class, include a weekly listening log, a vocabulary record, and a note-taking summary sheet.

It is important that students be exposed to as many examples from the broadcast media as possible. Students should be encouraged to listen to both radio and television news outside of class and use the photocopiable activity sheets to guide their listening.

Assessment

Assessing student performance and progress is an integral part of teaching. Tips on evaluating students during classroom activities are provided in the **Teacher's Book.**

ACKNOWLEDGMENTS

I dedicate this book to my parents.

I would like to thank everyone at Oxford University Press, particularly Chris Foley, Paul Riley, Ellen Kisslinger, Steve Maginn, Eleanor Barnes, Karen Brock, Bev Curran, and Anita Raducanu for their encouragement, patience, skill, wisdom, and hard work. I would also like to thank the management, teaching staff, and students of Athénée Français, Tokyo, for their help in developing and piloting the material in this book. In addition, thanks to the reviewers for their valuable comments on early versions of the manuscript.

Roger Barnard

TO THE STUDENT

This course is designed to help you take advantage of the news reports available to you in the broadcast media. It focuses on the skills you need to understand English language broadcasts and then talk about what you hear.

SUGGESTIONS

Here are some some ways you can make the most of the course:

- Try to relax when you listen.

- When you are listening for the main points of a story, try to listen for the gist, not every word.

- Don't focus on a word you don't know. You may understand it later in the story if you keep on listening.

- Don't be afraid to guess if you are unsure of something; we often have to guess when listening in everyday situations.

- Don't expect to understand everything after one or two listenings. Each time you hear the story you will understand a little bit more.

- Don't confuse "listening ability" with "remembering." We often understand something in our own language that we can't remember after a short time.

- Don't look at the **Extra Practice** section before doing the listening exercises. Your listening skills will improve faster, and the lessons will be more interesting if you wait.

- After listening to the stories, talk about them and share your reactions.

- Don't be afraid to make mistakes. Participate in discussions and listen to your classmates' ideas.

- Listen to the news outside of class. Try to use the skills you learn in class.

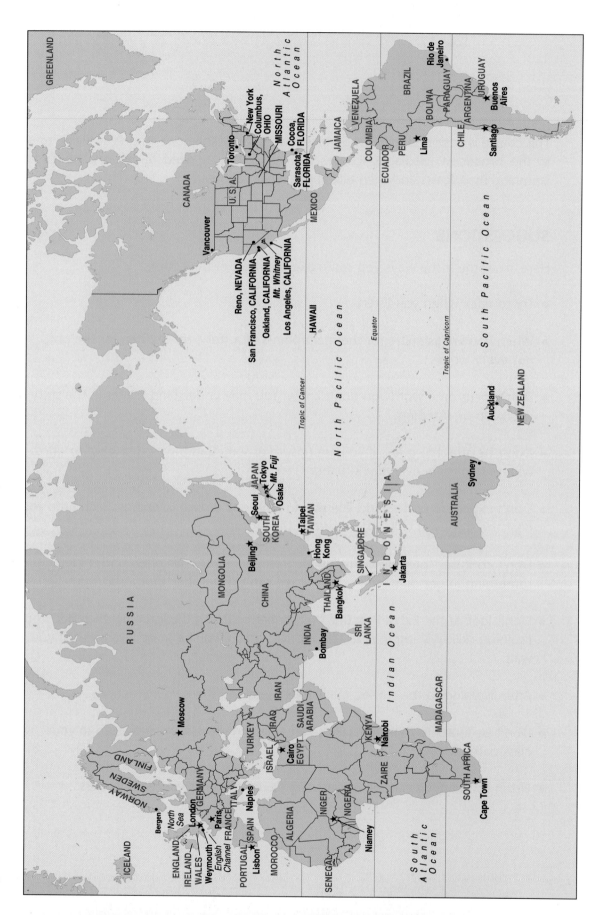

STORY 1

Dream Jackpot

▶ Tuning In

1 You are going to hear a story about a dream. Look at the picture. What do you think happened?

2 Use the words in the box to complete the sentences. The first one has been done for you.

1. ___*Hit the jackpot*___ means win a big prize.

2. If you _____ a place, you go toward it.

3. A _____ is a person who has a million dollars or more.

4. If you have _____ , you have a lot of it.

5. When you _____ , you sleep for a short time.

6. If something _____ , a lot of it comes out quickly.

pours out
take a nap
buckets of money
millionaire
hit the jackpot
head for

▶ Good News, Bad News

1 Two people are talking about the story. Listen to the story. Then check (✔) the best question.

Did you hear about the woman who dreamed of
☐ finding a lot of money?
☐ winning a lot of money?
☐ losing a lot of money?

Yes, and it came true, right?

2 Before you listen again, try to number the pictures in the order the events happened. Then listen and check your work. The first one has been done for you.

A. ☐

B. ☐

C. ☐

D. ☐

E. *1*

F. ☐

3 Listen to the story again. Then circle the correct information.
The first one has been done for you.

1. Mrs. Anderson lives in (Oakland)/ **Reno.**

2. She's **44** / **54** years old.

3. She has **5** / **6** children.

4. She has **18** / **19** grandchildren.

5. She's **a nurse** / **a nurse's assistant** in a hospital.

6. She arrived in Reno at **2 A.M.** / **2 P.M.**

7. She paid **$5** / **$3** for each try on the slot machine.

8. She won the **second** / **third** time she played.

▶ Signing Off

A Look at these types of dreams and write down
some true information about yourself.

YOU HAD A DREAM ABOUT
ALIENS, DEAR?
JUST GO BACK TO SLEEP.

Have you ever had a dream about...?

- the future, and it came true
- flying
- a famous person
- falling
- someone chasing you
- a strange house
- being worried
- finding money
- the sea

B Now work with a partner. Take turns talking about your dreams.

A: *Have you ever had a dream about...?*
B: | *No, I haven't. How about you?*
   |
   | *Yes, I have.* | *Last week/month/year,* |
   | | *About a year ago,* | *I had a dream about...*
   | | *When I was a child,* |

EXTRA
PRACTICE,
page 55

STORY 2
False Alarm

▶ Tuning In

1 You are going to hear a story about something that happened on a plane. Look at the picture. What do you think happened?

2 Use the words in the box to complete the questions.

1. What's a(n) _____ ?
   It's when a plane lands in a dangerous way.

2. What does _____ mean?
   It's another way of saying hurry.

3. What's a(n) _____ ?
   That's someone who looks after passengers on a plane.

4. What does a(n) _____ mean?
   Twelve.

5. What's a(n) _____ ?
   One meaning is a long narrow passage between rows of seats.

6. What does _____ mean?
   It's a warning that something dangerous is going to happen, but it doesn't.

> false alarm
>
> dozen
>
> aisle
>
> flight attendant
>
> crash landing
>
> rush

▶ **Good News, Bad News**

1 Listen to the story. Then check (✔) the best headline.

☐ **Wrong Message Played on Plane**

☐ 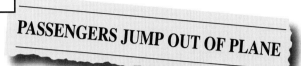 **PASSENGERS JUMP OUT OF PLANE**

☐  **TAPED MESSAGE SAVES PASSENGERS**

2 Before you listen again, read the sentences below. Then listen and number them in the order the events happened. The first one has been done for you.

☐ a. The message told the passengers they were going to land on water.

☐ b. The passengers heard a taped message.

| 1 | c. A plane took off in Portugal.

☐ d. A flight attendant then explained that it was a false alarm.

☐ e. The cabin crew rushed into the aisles.

☐ f. It told them to get their lifejackets.

☐ g. The plane started to cross the English Channel.

3 Listen to the story again. Then circle the correct answer for each question. The first one has been done for you.

1. How long did the passengers prepare for a crash landing?
   - (a.) For two minutes.
   - b. For twenty minutes.

2. When did the false alarm happen?
   - a. Wednesday morning.
   - b. Wednesday afternoon.

3. Where was the flight going?
   - a. To London.
   - b. To Lisbon.

4. How many passengers were there on the plane?
   - a. 103.
   - b. 113.

5. What was the flight number?
   - a. BA32.
   - b. VA32.

6. How many message tapes were there?
   - a. Less than 12.
   - b. More than 12.

▶ Signing Off

You are going on a 12-hour flight in a jumbo jet. You are going to fly alone in economy class. For each item, check (✔) which option you prefer. If you don't care, draw a dash (–) in both boxes. When you have finished, discuss your choices with a partner. Talk about your own ideas, too.

FLYING IS SO RELAXING, ISN'T IT?

1. ❏ a window seat   OR   ❏ an aisle seat
2. ❏ the smoking section   OR   ❏ the non-smoking section
3. ❏ a large movie screen   OR   ❏ a personal TV screen
4. ❏ a quiet neighbor   OR   ❏ a friendly, talkative neighbor
5. ❏ a female flight attendant   OR   ❏ a male flight attendant
6. ❏ the front of the plane   OR   ❏ the rear of the plane

> A: *Which do you prefer, a window seat or an aisle seat?*
> *I prefer a window seat. I can see out of the window.*
> *How about you?*
> B: *I don't care. Either is fine with me.*

EXTRA PRACTICE, page 56

STORY 3

A Fishy Story

▶ Tuning In

1 You are going to hear a story about fishing. Look at the picture. What do you think happened?

2 Match the beginning of each sentence with its ending. The first one has been done for you.

   _e_   1. **Discover** means the same as

         2. If you **swallow** something,

         3. One meaning of **incredible** is

         4. If you **bite** something,

         5. One meaning of **a spot** is

         6. **Jewelry** is

a. it goes from your mouth to your stomach.

b. difficult to believe.

c. sometimes made of gold or precious stones.

d. a place.

e. find.

f. you take hold of it with your teeth.

▶ Good News, Bad News

1 Listen to the story. Then check (✔) the best summary.

☐ It's about a woman who lost her earring while she was fishing.

☐ It's about a man who found his wife's earring in a fish.

☐ It's about a man who lost his earring in a fish.

2 Before you listen again, try to number the pictures in the order the events happened. Then listen and check your work.

A. ☐

B. ☐

C. ☐

D. ☐

E. ☐

F. ☐

3 Listen to the story again. Then circle the correct information.

1. Waldemar Andersen went fishing last **Wednesday / weekend.**

2. He went fishing **near / in** Bergen.

3. Bergen is in **Sweden / Norway.**

4. His wife had lost a **gold / silver** earring.

5. Andersen found the earring in the **mouth / stomach** of a fish.

6. He **knew / didn't know** that he was fishing from the same place where his wife had lost the earring.

▶ Signing Off

A Think of a story about losing something. Your story must be *100% true* or *100% false!* Use the questions below to help you.

Sample questions:

What did you lose?

Was it valuable?

Where did you lose it?

What were you doing when you lost it?

How did you feel when you lost it?

How did you lose it?

Did you get it back?

How did you get it back?

B When you are ready, your partner will ask you questions. He/She can use the questions in the box, as well as other questions. If your story is *true,* try to make your partner think it is *false.* If it is *false,* try to make your partner think it is *true.*

EXTRA PRACTICE, page 57

C After you finish answering, your partner should decide if your story is *true* or *false.*

STORY 4

A Long Trip

▶ Tuning In

1 You are going to hear a story about a trip. Look at the pictures.
What do you think happened?

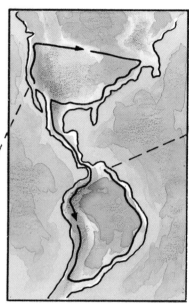

2 Use the words in the box to complete the sentences.

1. A(n) _____ is someone who works
for a company.

2. When you are traveling, the place you are heading for
is your _____ .

3. If you run faster, higher, or longer than anyone else
ever has, you set a new _____ .

4. A(n) _____ is a person who protects
a building.

5. One way _____ is to bring your own
lunch to work or school.

6. If you _____ , you stop traveling and
live in one place.

to save money
record
settle down
employee
security guard
destination

▶ Good News, Bad News

1 Listen to the story. Then check (✔) the best question.

Did you hear about the guy who
- ☐ cycled around the world?
- ☐ cycled around Africa?
- ☐ walked around the world?

Yes, he just got back, right?

2 Read the sentences below. Listen to the story, then check (✔)
True or **False**. The first one has been done for you.

	True	False
1. Masami Kono owned a supermarket.	☐	☑
2. He started his trip in Tokyo.	☐	☐
3. His final destination was in Africa.	☐	☐
4. He set a new Japanese bicycle trip record.	☐	☐
5. He spent all his savings during his trip.	☐	☐
6. He worked at a variety of jobs.	☐	☐
7. He usually slept in cheap hotels to save money.	☐	☐
8. He doesn't want to go on another long trip.	☐	☐

3 Listen to the story again. Then complete the answers, using the numbers in the box.

1. How old is Masami Kono?
   He's _____ .

2. How long did it take him to complete his trip?
   _____ years.

3. How many kilometers did he cycle?
   _____ kilometers.

4. How many continents did he cross?
   He traveled across _____ .

5. How much longer was his trip than the previous Japanese record?
   Over _____ kilometers.

6. How much money did he save for his trip?
   He saved ¥_____ .

34
5
17,000
1,000,000
8
59,464

▶ Signing Off

A You are going to travel around the world for at least three months. You can visit up to five countries. Look at the map on page viii to plan your route. Think about:

- how you will travel
- what you will take with you
- what you will do and see
- where you will sleep

B Get together with another student and ask each other about your plans.

> **Sample questions:**
> *Where are you going to go first/then/next/after that?*
> *How are you going to travel?*
> *What are you going to take with you?*
> *What do you want to do/see in (Egypt)?*
> *Where are you going to sleep?*

EXTRA PRACTICE, page 58

Having a Ball

▶ Tuning In

1 You are going to hear a story about some people who bought a new house. Look at the picture. What do you think happened?

2 Use the words in the box to complete the questions.

1. What does _____ mean?
   One meaning is hit or attack continuously.

2. What does _____ mean?
   It means connected with the law.

3. What kind of place is a(n) _____ ?
   It's a place where battles are fought.

4. What's a(n) _____ ?
   It's a person who builds houses and other buildings to sell.

5. What does _____ mean?
   It means to try to get money from someone in a court of law.

6. What is _____ ?
   It's facts or objects that help to prove something is or is not true.

> property
>   developer
>
> bombard
>
> war zone
>
> legal
>
> evidence
>
> to sue

▶ Good News, Bad News

1 Listen to the story. Then check (✔) the best headline.

☐

COUPLE SUES GOLFERS:
BACKYARD "A WAR ZONE"

☐

PROPERTY DEVELOPER SUES COUPLE

☐

COUPLE SUES PROPERTY DEVELOPER:
BACKYARD "A WAR ZONE"

2 Before you listen again, read the sentences below. Then listen and number them in the order the events happened.

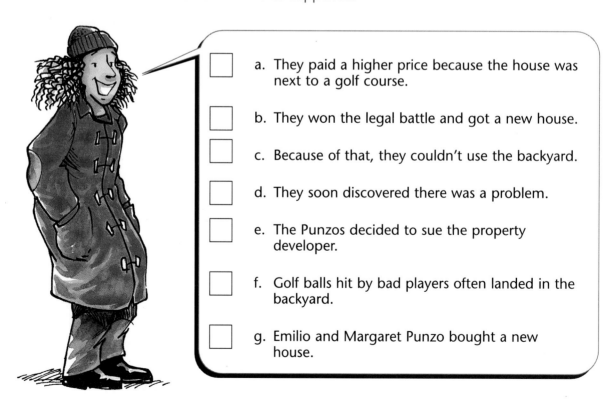

☐ a. They paid a higher price because the house was next to a golf course.

☐ b. They won the legal battle and got a new house.

☐ c. Because of that, they couldn't use the backyard.

☐ d. They soon discovered there was a problem.

☐ e. The Punzos decided to sue the property developer.

☐ f. Golf balls hit by bad players often landed in the backyard.

☐ g. Emilio and Margaret Punzo bought a new house.

3 Listen to the story again. Then circle the correct information.

1. The Punzos got a new house after a **four-year** / **five-year** legal battle.

2. The Punzos paid **$113,200** / **$132,000** for their house.

3. They paid an extra **$8,000** / **$18,000** because the house was next to a golf course.

4. They filled **a dozen** / **eight dozen** grocery bags with golf balls.

5. They collected more than **2,000** / **10,000** golf balls from their backyard.

▶ Signing Off

A What would your dream house or apartment be like? Look at the questions below and write down some ideas.

House
- Would it be old or new?
- Would the style be modern or traditional?
- How many floors would it have?
- How many rooms would it have?
- Would it have a big backyard?
- What kind of area or neighborhood would it be in?
- What would be special about it?

Apartment
- What floor would it be on?
- How many rooms would it have?
- Would it have a balcony?
- Would it have a roof garden?
- What kind of view would it have?

B Get together with another student and ask each other about your ideas.

EXTRA PRACTICE, page 59

STORY 6

Sea Mail

▶ Tuning In

1 You are going to hear a story about a girl who sent a letter.
Look at the picture. What's in the bottle? Why?

2 Use the words in the box to complete the sentences.

1. If you _____ something into something else,
   you push it in tightly.

2. A _____ town is a place that is next to the
   ocean.

3. If something is _____ onto a beach, it is
   carried there by the sea and left there.

4. A _____ is another way of saying a
   competition.

5. If you _____ something, you throw it gently.

6. If you _____ a picture, you put it in a border
   of wood, metal, or other materials.

contest
coastal
stuff
toss
frame
washed up

▶ Good News, Bad News

1 Listen to the story. Then check (✔) the best response to the question.

> **Did you hear about the American girl who put a message in a bottle?**

> **Oh, yes. Some kids found it**
> ☐ in Southampton, didn't they?
> ☐ near New York, didn't they?
> ☐ on an English beach, right?

2 Read the sentences below. Listen to the story, then check (✔) **True** or **False**.

	True	False
1. Kimberly Corbisiero tossed a bottle into the Atlantic Ocean.	☐	☐
2. She lives in Atlantic City.	☐	☐
3. It washed up three months later on the English coast.	☐	☐
4. Some English schoolgirls found it.	☐	☐
5. There was only a letter inside the bottle.	☐	☐
6. The letter said that Kimberly was in a contest.	☐	☐
7. The letter told whoever found the bottle to keep the dollar bill.	☐	☐
8. The students haven't written to Kimberly.	☐	☐

3 Listen to the story again. Then check (✔) the correct response to complete the interview with one of the schoolboys who found the bottle.

REPORTER: Where were you when you found the bottle, Dick?
DICK: ☐ On the beach. ☐ In a boat.

REPORTER: How far did the bottle travel?
DICK: ☐ 4,800 km. ☐ 3,800 km.

REPORTER: How far did it travel per day?
DICK: ☐ 150 km. ☐ 160 km.

REPORTER: What was in it?
DICK: ☐ A letter and a dollar bill. ☐ A letter, an envelope, and a dollar bill.

REPORTER: Did you send the letter back?
DICK: ☐ Yes. ☐ No.

REPORTER: Where is the dollar bill now?
DICK: ☐ In the school library. ☐ In our classroom.

▶ Signing Off

A Imagine that you and your partner are going to stuff a message into a bottle and throw it into the ocean. Write the message on a piece of paper. Remember to sign it.

B Put your message on the wall of the classroom.

C With your partner, go around the room and read the messages. Decide which ones are the most interesting, amusing, etc. Write your answers below.

(L.L. Bean is a mail order company for clothing and sporting goods located in Freeport, Maine, USA.)

Which message is...	Names of senders
• the most interesting?	_____
• the most amusing?	_____
• the strangest?	_____
• the most neatly written?	_____

EXTRA PRACTICE, page 60

Easy Come, Easy Go

▶ Tuning In

1 You are going to hear a story about someone who went shopping. Look at the picture. What do you think happened?

2 Match the beginning of each sentence with its ending.

_____ 1. If you are **accused of** something,

_____ 2. When someone is **arrested,**

_____ 3. If you **hire** someone,

_____ 4. **Cab** is

_____ 5. **Several** means

_____ 6. A **fare** is

a. another word for taxi.

b. the money you pay for a trip by bus, train, taxi, etc.

c. three or more.

d. someone says you have done something wrong.

e. you pay someone to do something.

f. he or she is caught by the police.

▶ Good News, Bad News

1 Listen to the story. Then check (✔) the best summary.

☐ It's about a taxi driver who robbed some stores.

☐ It's about a guy who stole a taxi and then went shopping.

☐ It's about a guy who robbed a bank, then went shopping by taxi.

2 Before you listen again, try to number the pictures in the order the events happened. Then listen and check your work.

A. ☐

B. ☐

C. ☐

D. ☐

E. ☐

F. ☐

3 Listen to the story again. Then circle the correct information.

1. The story happened in **California** / **Florida**.

2. It happened in **December** / **January**.

3. Willie Williams rode in a taxi for **more than an hour** / **less than an hour**.

4. Willie Williams is **27 years old** / **37 years old**.

5. He bought **a suitcase and a plane ticket** / **clothing and a plane ticket**.

6. The cab fare was **$26.70** / **$27.60**.

▶ Signing Off

A Imagine that you are the one millionth shopper at a department store and you receive a $500 gift certificate. You can decide how to spend it, but you must choose from the items in the pictures. Look at your choices.

B For each item you choose, write down the price. Also add information about the item, such as color and brand name. Be careful not to spend more than $500!

Item	Price	Color	Other information
jeans	$40	blue	Levi's 501

C Next, talk with other students in the class. Compare your lists and discuss your decisions. Which items are the most popular?

A: What would you buy?
B: I decided to buy...
   I would buy...
A: Me, too.
   Not me. I'd buy...

EXTRA PRACTICE, page 61

Best Commuter

▶ Tuning In

1 You're going to hear a story about going to work. Look at the pictures. Why do you think the man is being interviewed?

2 Use the words in the box to complete the sentences.

1. A(n) _____ is someone who travels to and from work or school every day.

2. How much time do you _____ traveling every day?

3. Some men grow a beard so that they don't have to _____ .

4. Corn flakes are the most popular kind of breakfast _____ .

5. If you _____ doing something, you try not to do it.

6. The _____ is the average amount of money people pay for food, clothing, housing, etc.

spend
cost of living
cereal
avoid
shave
commuter

▶ Good News, Bad News

1 Listen to the story. Then check (✔) the best question.

Did you hear about the man who
- ❏ spends hours traveling to work by train every day?
- ❏ spends hours driving to work every day?
- ❏ drives long-distance trains?

Yes, he must be happy when he gets home!

2 Read the sentences below. Listen to the story, then check (✔) **True** or **False**.

	True	False
1. Barry Haddow travels from Wales to London every day.	❏	❏
2. He has just won the "Commuter of the Year" competition.	❏	❏
3. The competition was organized by an early morning TV program.	❏	❏
4. Mr. Haddow won because his commute takes the longest time.	❏	❏
5. The commute takes about three hours each way.	❏	❏
6. He travels most of the way by taxi.	❏	❏
7. He doesn't like Wales, but it's cheap.	❏	❏
8. He won a rail vacation for himself and his family.	❏	❏

3 Listen to the story again. Then complete the interview with
Barry Haddow, using the information you hear in the story.

REPORTER: Congratulations on being named "Commuter of the Year," Barry.
HADDOW: Thank you.
REPORTER: Just a few questions. Exactly how far do you travel every day?
HADDOW: _____
REPORTER: That's a long way. And what time do you get up?
HADDOW: _____
REPORTER: That's pretty early! Do you have time for breakfast?
HADDOW: _____
REPORTER: Uh-huh. Now, why do you live in Wales?
HADDOW: _____
REPORTER: Why don't you want to live in London?
HADDOW: _____
REPORTER: I see. Well, Barry, thanks for coming to speak to us, and enjoy your vacation.

▶ Signing Off

A Popular activities on commuter trains (according
to a recent survey) are listed below in jumbled
order. With a partner, rank them from 1 to 5.

___ reading ads on the train
___ reading a book
___ staring out the window
___ sleeping
___ reading a newspaper

B Talk to another pair and see if they agree. Then,
turn to page 62 to see the survey results.

C Now talk about your commute with other students.

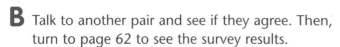

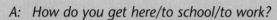

> A: How do you get here/to school/to work?
> B: | By train/bus/car/bicycle.
> | I walk.
> A: How long does it take?
> B: It takes about thirty minutes.
> A: What do you do during the commute?
> B: I listen to music.

EXTRA
PRACTICE,
page 62

A Drop-out

▶ Tuning In

1 You are going to hear a story about an accident. Look at the picture. What do you think happened?

2 Use the words in the box to complete the questions.

1. What does _____ mean?
   One meaning is to be hurt because of an accident.

2. What's a(n) _____ ?
   It's a kind of van that carries people to the hospital.

3. How do you _____ ?
   You stand by the side of the road and try to get a ride.

4. What's a(n) _____ ?
   It's a light bed used for carrying sick or injured people.

5. What does _____ mean?
   One meaning is not serious or not important.

6. What's a(n) _____ ?
   It's a car, bus, truck, etc. that carries things or people.

hitchhike
injured
minor
ambulance
stretcher
vehicle

Good News, Bad News

1 Listen to the story. Then check (✔) the best headline.

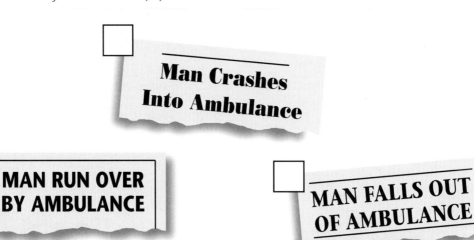

☐ **Man Crashes Into Ambulance**

☐ **MAN RUN OVER BY AMBULANCE**

☐ **MAN FALLS OUT OF AMBULANCE**

2 Before you listen again, read the sentences below. Then listen and number them in the order the events happened.

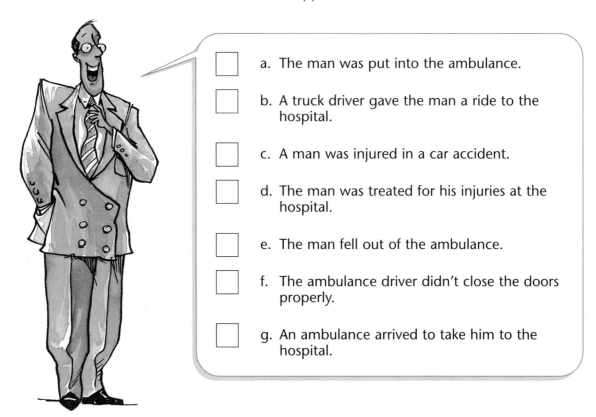

☐ a. The man was put into the ambulance.

☐ b. A truck driver gave the man a ride to the hospital.

☐ c. A man was injured in a car accident.

☐ d. The man was treated for his injuries at the hospital.

☐ e. The man fell out of the ambulance.

☐ f. The ambulance driver didn't close the doors properly.

☐ g. An ambulance arrived to take him to the hospital.

3 Listen to the story again. Then circle the correct answer for each question.

1. How old is Carmine Urciuolo?
   a. 23 years old.
   b. 33 years old.

2. Where did the traffic accident happen?
   a. Naples.
   b. Near Naples.

3. When did it happen?
   a. Wednesday afternoon.
   b. Thursday afternoon.

4. When did the ambulance driver notice Carmine was missing?
   a. At the hospital.
   b. Right away.

5. Was Carmine badly injured?
   a. Yes.
   b. No.

6. Was Carmine hurt in his fall from the ambulance?
   a. We don't know.
   b. Yes.

▶ Signing Off

A In groups of three, prepare a role play of an interview with Carmine Urciuolo at the hospital. One student will be Carmine and the other two will be reporters. Ask questions. You can use the questions below to help you.

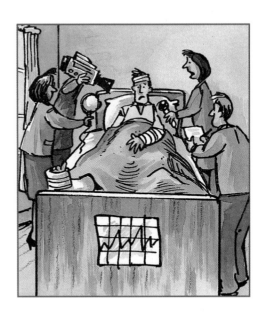

B Act out the role play two or three times, with a different student as Carmine each time.

Sample questions:

Can I ask you a few questions, Mr. Urciuolo?

How do you feel now?

How did the traffic accident happen?

Did you have to wait long for the ambulance?

How did you feel when you fell out?

How long did you spend hitchhiking?

What happened when you got to the hospital?

Are you going home by ambulance?

EXTRA PRACTICE, page 63

The Great Escape

▶ Tuning In

1 You are going to hear a story about an escape from prison.
Look at the picture. What do you think happened?

2 Match the beginning of each sentence with its ending.

_____ 1. One meaning of **prisoner** is

_____ 2. If someone is **armed**,

_____ 3. One meaning of **hover** is

_____ 4. **Surrender** means

_____ 5. If someone **serves a prison sentence,**

_____ 6. A **machine gun** is

a. he or she has a weapon such as a knife or gun.

b. stay in the air in the same place.

c. he or she stays in prison for a certain amount of time.

d. a gun that fires bullets quickly, one after the other.

e. stop fighting or trying to escape, and give up.

f. a person kept in prison for doing something wrong.

Good News, Bad News

1 Listen to the story. Then check (✔) the best summary.

☐ It's about a man who escaped from prison by helicopter.

☐ It's about two men who escaped from prison by helicopter.

☐ It's about a woman who escaped from prison by helicopter.

2 Before you listen again, try to number the pictures in the order the events happened. Then listen and check your work.

A. ☐

B. ☐

C. ☐

D. ☐

E. ☐

F. ☐

29

3 Listen to the story again. Then complete the summary of the story, using the numbers in the box.

____ -year-old Michel Vaujour escaped from prison when ____ people, including a woman of about ____ , flew over the prison in a helicopter and dropped a line down to him. At the time of his escape, he was serving an ____-year prison sentence for armed robbery. Vaujour has escaped from prison ____ times.

2
4
18
30
34

▶ Signing Off

A Imagine you are a prisoner and want to escape. Luckily, there are lots of old tunnels that the guards don't know about. Look at the diagram and draw a line showing your escape route. Don't let anyone see your book.

B Now work with a partner. Take turns describing the route you took. Listen carefully and draw your partner's route on your diagram. Use a dotted line or a different color. Don't look at each other's books.

C Compare your routes. Did you draw your partner's route correctly? Did you choose the same route? If not, whose route is shorter?

Freedom!

Start here   = blocked tunnel   ⊢───⊣ 10 meters

Useful language:

Turn left/right.

Go straight for about (10 meters).

Take the first/second/third tunnel on the left/right.

Turn left/right at the end.

Could you repeat that?

Did you say (10 meters)?

Was that (left)?

EXTRA PRACTICE, page 64

Better Late Than Never

▶ Tuning In

1 You are going to hear a story about some things that were stolen. Look at the pictures. What do you think happened?

2 Use the words in the box to complete the sentences.

1. A(n) _____ is someone who steals.

2. Another way to say *thing* is _____ .

3. If you _____ , you do something that you promised to do.

4. When you _____ a package, you open it by taking the paper off.

5. A person who is _____ has stopped working, usually because he or she has reached a certain age, for example, 60.

6. If you _____ something, you remember it.

keep your word
unwrap
recall
retired
item
thief

▶ Good News, Bad News

1 Listen to the story. Then check (✔) the best question.

Did you hear about the man who
- ❏ gave some things back after he stole them years ago?
- ❏ got some things back after he lost them years ago?
- ❏ got some things back after they were stolen years ago?

> **No, what happened?**

2 Read the sentences below. Listen to the story, then check (✔)
True or **False**.

	True	False
1. Mr. McGarry's camera and credit card were stolen.	❏	❏
2. They were stolen seven years earlier.	❏	❏
3. They were stolen while Mr. McGarry was in Ireland.	❏	❏
4. He was there on business.	❏	❏
5. The items were stolen from his hotel room.	❏	❏
6. Mr. McGarry was sleeping when the items were stolen.	❏	❏
7. The Irish police promised to find the items.	❏	❏
8. The police returned them last week.	❏	❏

3 Listen to the story again. Then complete the interview with William McGarry, using the information you hear in the story.

REPORTER: Could I ask you a few questions, Mr. McGarry?

MCGARRY: Sure, go right ahead.

REPORTER: Can I ask a few personal questions first? How old are you?

MCGARRY: _____

REPORTER: Are you retired?

MCGARRY: _____

REPORTER: And where do you live now?

MCGARRY: _____

REPORTER: OK. Now where was the hotel you were staying at when the things were stolen?

MCGARRY: _____

REPORTER: What did the police officer say when he took the report? Do you remember?

MCGARRY: _____

REPORTER: Finally, how did you feel when you opened the package?

MCGARRY: _____

▶ Signing Off

A Work in groups of four to six. In each group, one student is a police officer and collects one "stolen" item from each of the others. The items should be the same kind if possible, for example, watches, pens, or dictionaries, and should be placed so that *only the police officer can see them.*

B One by one, speak to the police officer and try to reclaim your stolen item. To get it back, you must describe it in detail and say at least three correct things about it.

Useful language:

What can I do for you? →	My watch was stolen this morning.
What make is it? →	It's a Swatch.
What's it made of? →	It's made of plastic.
What color is it? →	It has a white face with a yellow sun on it.
Is it new? →	No, it's about three years old.
Anything else? →	It shows the date, and it has a blue band.
Is this it? →	Yes! Thank you!

EXTRA PRACTICE, page 65

Come Fly With Me

▶ Tuning In

1 You are going to hear a story about a young girl. Look at the picture. What do you think happened?

2 Use the words in the box to complete the questions.

1. What's a(n) _____ ?
   It's something you fly on the end of a string.

2. When does a plane _____ ?
   When it touches the ground at the end of a flight.

3. What does _____ mean?
   It means to stop holding something.

4. What's the meaning of _____ ?
   One meaning is avoid hitting something.

5. What's another way of saying _____ ?
   At once or right away.

6. What's another word for _____ ?
   Frightened.

| miss |
| land |
| immediately |
| let go |
| scared |
| kite |

▶ Good News, Bad News

1 Listen to the story. Then check (✔) the best headline.

☐

PLANE CRASHES AFTER HITTING KITE

☐

KITE TAKES GIRL FOR A RIDE

☐

GIRL SERIOUSLY HURT IN KITE ACCIDENT

2 Before you listen again, try to number the pictures in the order the events happened. Then listen and check your work.

A. ☐

B. ☐

C. ☐

D. ☐

E. ☐

F. ☐

3 Listen to the story again. Then circle the correct answer for
each question.

1. How old is DeAndra Anrig?
   a. Seven years old.   b. Eight years old.

2. Where is the park?
   a. South of San Francisco.   b. North of San Francisco.

3. What kind of plane was it?
   a. Single-engine.   b. Twin-engine.

4. How far was she carried?
   a. Thirteen meters.   b. Thirty meters.

5. When was she taken to the hospital?
   a. Right after the accident. b. A while after the accident.

6. Was she scared when she was in the air?
   a. Yes.   b. No.

▶ Signing Off

A Look at this *Calvin and Hobbes* comic strip. How old is Calvin (the boy)?
What's he doing? What happens? Do you think he's hurt?

B Think about an accident or near-accident you had when you were a
child. Write notes below. When you are ready, exchange stories with
a partner. If you prefer, you can talk about a friend or relative.

- How old were you?   _____
- Where were you?   _____
- What were you doing?   _____
- What happened?   _____
- Were you hurt?   _____

EXTRA
PRACTICE,
page 66

Stranger Than Fiction

▶ Tuning In

1 You are going to hear a story about strange things that are taking place in an American house. Look at the picture. What do you see happening?

2 Match the beginning of each sentence with its ending.

____ 1. If something **overturns**,

____ 2. A **faucet** is used to

____ 3. If something is **splattered** on a surface,

____ 4. A **news conference** is

____ 5. If something is **scary**,

____ 6. A **specialist** is

a. it is frightening.

b. a meeting where news reporters ask questions.

c. an expert in something.

d. turn water on and off at a sink.

e. it turns on its side or upside down.

f. small amounts of it are splashed over a wide area.

Good News, Bad News

1 Listen to the story. Then check (✔) the best summary.

It's about a girl who causes things to disappear in her home.

It's about a girl who causes things to fly around in her home.

It's about a girl who flies around in her home.

2 Read the sentences below. Listen to the story, then check (✔)
True or **False**.

	True	False
1. The Resch family lives in Columbus, Ohio.	☐	☐
2. Strange things have been happening in their home for about a year.	☐	☐
3. Tina Resch is a teenager.	☐	☐
4. Strange things happen only when Tina is in the living room.	☐	☐
5. A reporter who was visiting the house saw a chair overturn.	☐	☐
6. The reporter didn't know why the chair overturned.	☐	☐
7. Tina is very frightened by what is happening.	☐	☐
8. Tina wants the strange things to continue.	☐	☐

3 Listen to the story again. Then circle the correct information.

1. According to the story, lights and water faucets have turned themselves **on** / **off**.

2. Eggs have splattered against the kitchen **walls** / **ceiling**.

3. Telephones have **risen** / **fallen** from tables.

4. The news conference was on Thursday **morning** / **afternoon**.

5. Tina **was** / **wasn't** next to the chair when it overturned during the news conference.

6. Tina's parents have taken her to **several** / **seven** specialists.

▶ Signing Off

A Some people believe in ghosts, ESP,* and UFOs.** What do students in your class think? Talk to five classmates. Find out their answers to the questions below. Write their names in the chart in the correct columns.

	Yes	No	Not sure
Do you believe in ghosts?			
Do you believe in ESP?			
Do you believe in UFOs?			
Have you ever seen a UFO?			
Do you think there is life on other planets?			

*ESP (Extrasensory Perception): The ability to sense things that can't be perceived by the five senses (sight, sound, touch, smell, taste).

**UFO (Unidentified Flying Object): Something seen in the sky that cannot be explained by science; a flying saucer.

B In small groups, compare your information.

> A: How many people said they believe in (UFOs)?
> B: I talked to five people. One person does not believe in (UFOs), one person does, and three people are not sure.
> C: (Ken) believes in (UFOs) because...

▶ EXTRA PRACTICE, page 67

Chain Smoker

▶ Tuning In

1 You are going to hear a story about smoking. Look at the picture. What do you think happened?

2 Use the words in the box to complete the sentences.

1. If you _____ , you stop doing something that's bad for you.

2. A(n) _____ is someone who smokes one cigarette after another without a break.

3. If an idea _____ , it is successful.

4. _____ is an Asian health treatment using needles.

5. When you practice _____ , you stay quiet and calm for a long time.

6. If you _____ someone to do something, you get him or her to do it by giving a good reason.

> **works**
>
> **kick a habit**
>
> **meditation**
>
> **chain smoker**
>
> **persuade**
>
> **acupuncture**

Good News, Bad News

1 Listen to the story. Then check (✔) the best headline.

☐ Friends chain man to sofa for weeks

☐ **MAN CHAIN SMOKES FOR WEEKS**

☐ MAN CHAINS HIMSELF TO SOFA FOR WEEKS

2 Before you listen again, read the sentences below. Then listen and number them in the order the events happen.

☐ a. Then his friends unchained him.

☐ b. Thomas Warren had been a smoker for 20 years.

☐ c. His friends chained him up in his living room.

☐ d. He celebrated by taking a run.

☐ e. He decided to try to stop smoking.

☐ f. After three weeks he had kicked the habit.

☐ g. He persuaded his friends to help him.

3 Listen to the story again. Then complete the interview with Thomas Warren, using the information you hear in the story.

REPORTER: Now that you're a free man, Mr. Warren, how do you feel?

WARREN: Great, just great.

REPORTER: How long were you a smoker?

WARREN: _____

REPORTER: Did you try to give up smoking before?

WARREN: _____

REPORTER: What did you try?

WARREN: _____

REPORTER: How many cigarettes were you smoking a day before you stopped?

WARREN: _____

REPORTER: And how long was your celebration run?

WARREN: _____

REPORTER: Are you going to start smoking again?

WARREN: _____

▶ Signing Off

Some people have these habits:

- oversleeping
- watching too much TV
- eating a lot of sweets and cakes
- being late for appointments
- biting their fingernails
- *your own idea* _____

(See page 68 for an explanation of how the wake-up system works.)

In groups of three or four, think of some amusing and unusual ways of helping someone to kick these habits.

A: How can someone stop watching a lot of TV?
B: Well, he/she can paint half of the TV screen black.
can put the TV in the bathroom.
could stay out all the time.
could throw away the remote control.

EXTRA PRACTICE, page 68

STORY 15

Never Too Old

▶ Tuning In

1 You are going to hear a story about an active woman. Look at the picture. What is the woman doing? Why?

2 Use the words in the box to complete the questions.

1. How many states are there in the _____?
   Forty-eight (Alaska and Hawaii aren't included).

2. What does the _____ Prime Minister mean?
   It means he or she is no longer alive.

3. How do you feel if you suffer from _____?
   You often feel very sad and don't want to do anything.

4. What does _____ mean?
   One meaning is exercising a lot to prepare physically for something.

5. What does _____ mean?
   It means you become strong again.

6. What's a _____?
   It's the number you get when you add some numbers together.

> regain your strength
>
> continental United States
>
> depression
>
> total
>
> training
>
> late

▶ Good News, Bad News

1 Listen to the story. Then check (✔) the best headline.

☐
91-YEAR-OLD TO CLIMB MT. FUJI

☐
91-YEAR-OLD CLIMBS MT. FUJI

☐
91-YEAR-OLD CLIMBS MT. WHITNEY

2 Before you listen again, try to number the pictures in the order the events happened. Then listen and check your work.

A. ☐

B. ☐

C. ☐

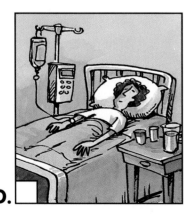

D. ☐

E. ☐

F. ☐

3 Listen to the story again. Then circle the correct answer for each question.

1. How high is Mt. Fuji?
    a. 3,776 meters.   b. 3,767 meters.
2. How high is Mt. Whitney?
    a. 4,412 meters.   b. 4,420 meters.
3. When did Ms. Crooks last climb Mt. Whitney?
    a. When she was 87.   b. When she was 89.
4. How many days is she going to spend climbing Mt. Fuji?
    a. Two days.   b. Three days.
5. How many times did she climb 60 steps on Monday?
    a. 15.   b. 50.
6. How many mountains has she climbed since her 65th birthday?
    a. 87.   b. 97.

▶ Signing Off

A Many senior citizens (people over 65) are quite active and enjoy life. Write down a few advantages and disadvantages of being a senior citizen. Then discuss your ideas in small groups.

Advantages	Disadvantages
you can get a seat on a bus or a train	_you're too tired to go to parties every night_
_____	_____
_____	_____
_____	_____

Useful language:

If you are a senior citizen...

(maybe) | *you don't have to...*
you don't need to...
you can...

(maybe) | *you have to...*
you can't...
it's difficult to...

B By yourself, take a minute to think about a senior citizen you know personally or you know about from the media. When you are ready, get into groups again and take turns telling each other about the person.

EXTRA PRACTICE, page 69

The Longest Wait

▶ Tuning In

1 You are going to hear a story about someone waiting for something.
Look at the picture. What do you think the people are waiting for?

2 Match the beginning of each sentence with its ending.

_____ 1. A **department store**

_____ 2. There are one hundred **pence**

_____ 3. An **electrician**

_____ 4. An **annual** event happens

_____ 5. If you **pace up and down,**

_____ 6. The **Guinness Book of Records** contains some really strange facts,

a. in an English pound.

b. you walk back and forth.

c. for example, the size of the largest pizza ever made.

d. is a large store with separate sections for selling many kinds of goods.

e. once a year.

f. is someone who installs and repairs electrical equipment.

Good News, Bad News

1 Listen to the story. Then check (✔) the best summary.

☐ It's about a young guy who waited a long time to buy something expensive.

☐ It's about a young guy who waited a long time to apply for a job at a department store.

☐ It's about a young guy who waited a long time for a sale to begin.

2 Read the sentences below. Listen to the story, then check (✔)
True or **False**.

	True	False
1. Phil Illsley waited for a department store sale.	☐	☐
2. He waited for more than two weeks.	☐	☐
3. He was the first person allowed in the sale.	☐	☐
4. It took him a long time in the store to decide what to buy.	☐	☐
5. He bought a pen and pencil set at the sale.	☐	☐
6. Phil Illsley said he wanted to set a new world record.	☐	☐
7. He spent most of his time sleeping.	☐	☐
8. He slept in a sleeping bag.	☐	☐

3 Listen to the story again. Then circle the correct information.

1. Phil Illsley shopped at the sale on **Tuesday** / **Wednesday**.
2. He saved **65** / **75** pence.
3. Phil Illsley is an **electrician** / **optician**.
4. The item he bought cost **£1.50** / **£1.15**.
5. He waited for **316** / **360** hours.
6. The previous record for the longest wait was **302** / **312** hours, 40 minutes.

▶ Signing Off

A Look at these records from the Guinness Book of Records. Work in groups and try to guess the missing information. Fill in your guesses. When you have finished, turn to page 70 to find out the correct information. The group that guesses an item correctly or is the closest, wins a point. The group with the most points wins.

a. Susan Montgomery Williams of California blew the biggest bubble-gum bubble in 1994. It was _____ centimeters in diameter.

b. Yogesh Sharma shook hands with _____ different people in eight hours in Gwalior, India, in 1996.

c. Ashrita Furman of New York balanced _____ beer glasses on his chin in 1996.

d. The tallest snowman was made in Yamagata, Japan, in 1995. It was _____ meters tall.

B In groups, try to think of new kinds of records for the Guinness Book of Records. The stranger the better!

Examples:
Eating the most slices of pizza at one sitting.
Knitting the largest sweater.
Standing on one leg for the longest time.

EXTRA PRACTICE, page 70

Romeo, Romeo

▶ Tuning In

1 You are going to hear a romantic story. Look at the picture.
What do you think happened?

2 Use the words in the box to complete the sentences.

1. The _____ is the full-length movie at
   a movie theater.

2. A _____ movie is one without speaking.

3. If you are _____ someone, you are
   faithful to him or her.

4. _____ are words written at the
   bottom of the movie screen.

5. When you _____ someone, you go
   out regularly together.

6. If you _____ someone, you ask him
   or her to marry you.

> subtitles
>
> date
>
> true to
>
> main feature
>
> propose to
>
> silent

▶ Good News, Bad News

1 Listen to the story. Then check (✔) the best question.

Did you hear about the man who
- ❏ proposed to a movie star?
- ❏ proposed to his girlfriend from the movie screen?
- ❏ got married in a movie theater?

Yeah, wasn't it romantic!

2 Before you listen again, try to number the pictures in the order the events happened. Then listen and check your work.

A.

B.

C.

D.

E.

F.

3 Listen to the story again. Then complete the interview with Beth Corey, using the information you hear in the story.

REPORTER: Beth, I understand both you and Kevin are in your twenties.

BETH: That's right. We're both 25.

REPORTER: How long have you been dating?

BETH: _____

REPORTER: Tell me about the movie. How many people were in it?

BETH: _____

REPORTER: How long did Kevin spend making the film, do you know?

BETH: _____

REPORTER: And how long was the film?

BETH: _____

REPORTER: How did you feel when you saw Kevin on the screen?

BETH: _____

REPORTER: Do you remember exactly what the subtitles said?

BETH: _____

▶ Signing Off

When you hear the word "romantic," do you think of red roses or yellow tulips? Paris in spring or Rome in summer? First, complete the list below. Then, with a partner, compare your ideas. Give examples and reasons.

Think of a romantic…

- color   _____

- kind of food   _____

- foreign city   _____

- city in your country _____

- movie (title)   _____

- actor/actress   _____

- song   _____

- singer   _____

EXTRA PRACTICE, page 71

Barney or Blue?

▶ Tuning In

1 You are going to hear a story about a pet. Look at the picture.
What do you think happened?

2 Use the words in the box to complete the questions.

1. When is a noise _____ ?
   When it's high-pitched and unpleasant.

2. What happens if you _____ somebody?
   You don't pay attention to him or her.

3. What's a _____ ?
   A person who breaks into buildings to steal things.

4. What happens if you _____ a baby's foot?
   The baby laughs, usually!

5. What does _____ someone mean?
   It means identify or know someone you have seen or met before.

6. What does it mean if someone is a _____ criminal?
   It means the police think the person is guilty, but they are not sure yet.

burglar
suspected
tickle
recognize
piercing
ignore

Good News, Bad News

1 Listen to the story. Then check (✔) the best response to the question.

I heard part of it.

- [ ] A woman was sent to jail for stealing a parrot, wasn't she?
- [ ] A parrot was sent to jail for burglary, right?
- [ ] A parrot sent a man to jail, right?

Did you hear the story on the news about the parrot?

2 Read the sentences below. Listen to the story, then check (✔) **True** or **False**.

	True	False
1. Ms. Morgans' parrot was stolen.	☐	☐
2. The police found a parrot in Eric Buckley's home.	☐	☐
3. The police thought Eric Buckley stole the parrot.	☐	☐
4. In court, Buckley said the parrot was his pet named Barney.	☐	☐
5. Ms. Morgans said that the parrot was her pet and that its name was Blue.	☐	☐
6. The parrot flew into the courtroom.	☐	☐
7. The parrot flew straight to Ms. Morgans.	☐	☐
8. The parrot squawked its own name, "Blue."	☐	☐

3 Listen to the story again. Then circle the correct answer for each question.

1. Where did the story happen?
   a. In the United States.   b. In England.
2. What kind of parrot was stolen?
   a. African gray.   b. Amazon.
3. How much is he worth?
   a. $1,000.   b. $10,000.
4. Who is 27 years old?
   a. Eric Buckley.   b. Georgina Morgans.
5. Who whistled in the courtroom?
   a. The parrot.   b. Eric Buckley.
6. Who tickled the parrot under the beak?
   a. Georgina Morgans.   b. Eric Buckley.

▶ Signing Off

A Take a minute to think about a pet you have or have had. It can also be a friend's or a relative's pet. Then write answers to the questions below.

- What kind of animal is (was) it?
- What is (was) its name?
- What does (did) it look like?
- How long have you had (did you have) it?
- What does (did) it like to do?
- Does (Did) it ever do anything funny or interesting?

B Now, in pairs, interview each other about your pets. Use the questions above. Add questions of your own.

> A: Do you have a pet?
> B: | Yes, I do.
> | No, but I used to have...
> | No, but my (friend) has a...

EXTRA PRACTICE, page 72

C Decide whose pet has done the funniest or most interesting thing.

Dream Jackpot

(pages 1–3)

 First, try to write in the missing words in the blanks below. Then listen and check your work.

EXTRA
PRACTICE

A woman from Oakland, California, dreamed of money (1) _____ of a slot machine, then drove to Nevada and hit the $1 million slot machine (2) _____ .

Fifty-four-year-old Pearl Anderson drove to Nevada in the (3) _____ of the night. "I (4) _____ in the afternoon before I went to work, and dreamed of (5) _____ pouring out of the machine. I told my (6) _____ about it when he came home and he told me to go to Reno."

Anderson has five children and 18 (7) _____ , and works evenings as a nurse's (8) _____ at a hospital. She left for Reno after work, arrived at 2 A.M., and (9) _____ the slot machines at the Club Cal Nueva.

On her second try at the "$3 (10) _____ slot machine," five sevens appeared on the register, bells rang, and buzzers (11) _____ , and the crowd clapped and (12) _____ .

husband	pouring out	millionaire
headed straight for	took a nap	jackpot
went off	grandchildren	cheered
buckets of money	middle	assistant

STORY 2

False Alarm

(pages 4–6)

EXTRA
PRACTICE

First, try to write in the missing words in the blanks below. Then listen and check your work.

For two minutes on Wednesday afternoon, (1) _____ aboard a British Airways flight from Portugal to London prepared for a (2) _____ in the English Channel.

"This is an (3) _____ ," said a taped message over the in-flight loudspeaker. The message then told passengers they were going to land on water. It told them to get their (4) _____ from under their seats and wait for further (5) _____ from the cabin crew.

The 103 passengers on flight BA32 were very frightened when the cabin crew (6) _____ into the (7) _____ . A (8) _____ then told everyone that it was a (9) _____ . She had pushed the wrong button, she said.

Out of more than a (10) _____ tapes — from announcing takeoff to selling duty-free alcohol — the flight attendant had made a (11) _____ and chosen the message that prepares passengers for a crash landing on water, a BA (12) _____ explained later.

rushed	emergency	passengers
spokesperson	lifejackets	instructions
crash landing	mistake	dozen
flight attendant	aisles	false alarm

A Fishy Story

(pages 7–9)

 First, try to write in the missing words in the blanks below. Then listen and check your work.

Waldemar Andersen went fishing last (1) _____ near the Norwegian city of Bergen and found the gold earring his wife had lost in the North Sea a week previously. He (2) _____ the earring in the (3) _____ of a cod fish.

Mrs. Andersen lost her earring two weeks (4) _____ while walking by the sea. Then last Saturday, her husband went fishing in the same place. He caught a fish and took it home. While he was (5) _____ it, he discovered his wife's earring inside. "I couldn't (6) _____ my eyes," he said.

Andersen's wife, Ragnhild, had this to say: "Think of all the fish swimming around there and that the same cod that (7) _____ my earring should (8) _____ on my husband's fishing hook a week later. It's (9) _____ ."

Andersen said he had not (10) _____ he was fishing from the (11) _____ where his wife lost the piece of (12) _____ .

swallowed	stomach	ago
discovered	spot	realized
cleaning	believe	incredible
jewelry	bite	weekend

STORY 4
A Long Trip
(pages 10–12)

EXTRA
PRACTICE

First, try to write in the missing words in the blanks below. Then listen and check your work.

A 34-year-old man recently returned home after traveling around the world for eight years by bicycle.

Masami Kono, a former supermarket (1) _____ , started from Osaka and cycled 59,464 kilometers in five (2) _____ — Australia, North and South America, Europe, and Africa — before reaching his final (3) _____ , Niamey, Niger, in Africa.

He beat the previous Japanese (4) _____ for a bicycle trip by over 17,000 kilometers.

After (5) _____ the ¥1,000,000 he had saved for the journey, Kono had to work at (6) _____ jobs along the way. He earned money as a judo teacher, a waiter, a fisherman, a (7) _____ , and a gardener. He usually camped in a tent (8) _____ .

When Kono was asked why he (9) _____ to cycle around the world, he said that before he got married and (10) _____ he wanted to do something that he could tell his children about. But he (11) _____ that after working for a while, he would like to try one more (12) _____ .

to save money	record	employee
settled down	destination	added
spending	various	decided
security guard	continents	journey

STORY 5

Having a Ball

(pages 13–15)

 First, try to write in the missing words in the blanks below. Then listen and check your work.

A couple, whose home and backyard were (1) _____ with thousands of mis-hit golf balls, has won a new house after a five-year (2) _____ battle.

Emilio and Margaret Punzo paid $132,000 for their "dream home" in San Ramon near San Francisco. The price even (3) _____ an extra $8,000 charge because the house was next to a golf course.

After moving in, they soon discovered the (4) _____ — golf balls from bad players. They were unable to use their backyard because it was "like a (5) _____ ," according to Mr. Punzo.

They (6) _____ the (7) _____ who sold them the house, and produced as (8) _____ golf balls that had (9) _____ in their backyard. They showed the judge a dozen (10) _____ filled with more than 2,000 balls.

The Punzos won, and the judge told the property developer to pay for another house for them. They are (11) _____ moving into their new house soon and (12) _____ in the backyard.

looking forward to	included	bombarded
property developer	evidence	relaxing
grocery bags	war zone	legal
sued	drawback	landed

STORY 6
Sea Mail

(pages 16–18)

EXTRA
PRACTICE

First, try to write in the missing words in the
blanks below. Then listen and check your work.

American schoolgirl Kimberly Corbisiero could have a big future in express mail.

Nine-year-old Kimberly (1) _____ a message in a bottle and
(2) _____ it into the Atlantic Ocean near her home in Staten Island,
New York, on December 10th. Just one month later, it (3) _____ ,
4,800 kilometers away, on the south coast of England.

The bottle was found by three schoolboys during a school trip near the
(4) _____ town of Weymouth. The bottle had traveled about 160 km
a day. (5) _____ was a letter, an (6) _____ , and a
dollar bill. The letter read: "If you find this letter, please mail it back to me and
(7) _____ the dollar. I am in a (8) _____ . Please tell
me where you (9) _____ this letter."

The students at St. Edward's, a boys' school near Southampton, have already sent Kimberly
a (10) _____ — through the (11) _____ mail.
Kimberly won't get her letter back, though. Both the letter and the dollar bill have been
(12) _____ and hung in the school library.

Inside	stuffed	washed up
coastal	keep	reply
regular	found	tossed
envelope	framed	contest

STORY 7

Easy Come, Easy Go

(pages 19–21)

 First, try to write in the missing words in the blanks below. Then listen and check your work.

EXTRA PRACTICE

A man has been (1) _____ robbing a bank in Sarasota, Florida.

(2) _____ , he wanted to do some Christmas shopping, so he

(3) _____ a taxi outside the bank and rode from store to store for

(4) _____ an hour before he was (5) _____ .

After getting into the (6) _____ , 37-year-old Willie Carroll Williams
first stopped at the Sarasota Airport to buy plane tickets, and then visited

(7) _____ shopping centers.

According to police officers who arrested Williams on Monday, the cab was filled with
shopping bags (8) _____ shirts, shoes, and pants. At the
(9) _____ of his arrest, Williams' cab (10) _____
was $26.70.

The cab driver said that during the (11) _____ Williams told him,
"When you've got the money, you might as well spend it." The driver added that
Williams (12) _____ to be having a good time.

seemed	several	Apparently
arrested	cab	hired
ride	time	more than
fare	containing	accused of

Best Commuter

(pages 22–24)

EXTRA PRACTICE First, try to write in the missing words in the blanks below. Then listen and check your work.

Barry Haddow, who travels 547 kilometers from Wales to London and back each day, has been named "(1) _____ of the Year" by British Rail.

An early morning radio program (2) _____ the competition to find the person who commutes the (3) _____ every day. Haddow, who (4) _____ more than six hours traveling each day, was the winner.

He saves time by (5) _____ the night before, gets up before six o'clock, and has (6) _____ for breakfast (7) _____ cooking. A high-speed train takes him to London at 200 kilometers an hour. In London, he (8) _____ a taxi to get to his office, where he works as an (9) _____ in the oil industry.

Why does he do it? "I love Wales, the golf, the low (10) _____ . London is noisy and dirty, the people are (11) _____ , and the houses are expensive."

Haddow's prize was a rail (12) _____ for himself, his wife, and their two children.

to avoid	organized	Commuter
shaving	engineer	vacation
cost of living	unfriendly	spends
cereal	jumps into	furthest

ANSWERS TO **Signing Off A**, p. 24
1 reading a book (35%)
2 reading ads on the train (33%)
3 staring out the window (26%)
4 sleeping/reading a newspaper (both 24%)

STORY 9

A Drop-out

(pages 25–27)

 First, try to write in the missing words in the blanks below. Then listen and check your work.

EXTRA PRACTICE

According to Italian newspapers, an (1) _____ man fell out of the back of an (2) _____ onto the road and had to (3) _____ the rest of the way to the hospital.

Twenty-three-year-old Carmine Urciuolo was injured in a (4) _____ accident near Naples on Thursday afternoon. An ambulance soon arrived at the (5) _____ , and Carmine was put onto a (6) _____ and into the ambulance. While the ambulance was taking him to the (7) _____ hospital, Urciuolo and the stretcher he was lying on fell out of the ambulance. Apparently, the driver had not correctly closed the doors of the (8) _____ .

The driver didn't realize that he had lost the patient until the ambulance (9) _____ the hospital. He was quite surprised to find no one inside when he opened the ambulance doors outside the (10) _____ department.

A (11) _____ truck driver gave Urciuolo a ride to the hospital, where he was treated for (12) _____ injuries. The newspapers did not say which of the injuries were from the car accident or which were from the fall from the ambulance.

passing	injured	nearest
hitchhike	stretcher	reached
minor	emergency	scene
vehicle	ambulance	traffic

The Great Escape

(pages 28–30)

First, try to write in the missing words in the blanks below. Then listen and check your work.

A helicopter piloted by a woman lifted a (1) _____ from a
(2) _____ of La Santé Prison in Paris on Monday and flew him out.

The escaped prisoner was (3) _____ Michel Vaujour, 34, who was found
guilty of (4) _____ robbery last year. He was (5) _____
an 18-year sentence and this was his fourth escape from prison.

Police said that a second prisoner (6) _____ at the last minute not to join
Vaujour and (7) _____ .

According to police, the helicopter flew into the prison at about 10:45 A.M. and
(8) _____ over a prison building. Two people were
(9) _____ the aircraft, one armed with a (10) _____ .
They dropped a line to Vaujour and then flew away.

A spokesperson for Air Continent, who (11) _____ the helicopter, said it
had been (12) _____ by a woman about 30 years old.

hovered	serving	rooftop
identified as	own	aboard
machine gun	rented	prisoner
surrendered	armed	decided

Better Late Than Never

(pages 31–33)

First, try to write in the missing words in the blanks below. Then listen and check your work.

EXTRA PRACTICE

It took 17 years, but William McGarry (1) _____ got his camera and driver's license back.

(2) _____ in Ireland stole McGarry's camera and driver's
(3) _____ while the American was traveling through the country on vacation. The items were stolen from McGarry's (4) _____ car while he, his wife, and children were taking a nap in their hotel near Shannon Airport. At the time, Irish police (5) _____ they would find and return the
(6) _____ . Last week they (7) _____ .

McGarry (8) _____ a package that arrived in the mail from County Clare, Ireland, and pulled out the 35mm camera and license he had lost 17 years
(9) _____ . Seventy-two-year-old Mr. McGarry, who is
(10) _____ and lives in Cocoa, Florida, said that it was "just like Christmas."

McGarry (11) _____ that when police sergeant D.A. Foley took the
(12) _____ on the stolen items after the robbery, he said, "We'll find them for you."

recalled	Thieves	earlier
retired	unwrapped	license
kept their word	rental	report
finally	promised	items

Come Fly With Me

(pages 34–36)

EXTRA
PRACTICE

First, try to write in the missing words in the blanks below. Then listen and check your work.

A child flying a (1) _____ is a common sight in the

(2) _____ month of March, but not a kite flying a child.

As eight-year-old DeAndra Anrig was flying her new kite in a park south of San Francisco

on Sunday, a (3) _____ plane that was preparing to

(4) _____ at nearby Palo Alto Airport caught the kite's nylon string

and (5) _____ the child into the air. DeAndra was carried about

30 meters before she (6) _____ , fell to the ground, and just

(7) _____ a tree.

The girl was (8) _____ taken to a nearby hospital, but doctors said that

she was not (9) _____ hurt. The plane landed safely although one wing

was slightly (10) _____ .

What had DeAndra thought about during her (11) _____ flight?

"I wasn't thinking anything except how (12) _____ I was."

twin-engine	kite	lifted
let go	immediately	brief
scared	damaged	windy
land	seriously	missed

STORY 13

Stranger Than Fiction

(pages 37–39)

 First, try to write in the missing words in the blanks below. Then listen and check your work.

EXTRA PRACTICE

A family wants someone to explain why objects fly through the air and furniture
(1) _____ in their Columbus, Ohio, home.

John and Joan Resch said that since Saturday strange things have happened whenever
their (2) _____ daughter, Tina, is in the house. Some examples?
Lights and water (3) _____ have turned themselves on, eggs have
(4) _____ against the kitchen walls, and telephones have
(5) _____ from tables.

At a (6) _____ at the Resch home Thursday afternoon, one
(7) _____ said she saw a chair overturn as 14-year-old Tina entered
from the (8) _____ side of the room. The reporter could not explain
the movement.

Tina said the strange (9) _____ didn't really frighten her. "It's just a little
(10) _____ when things are flying around. I don't feel anything, but
I wish it would stop. I still don't (11) _____ things like this happen."

Tina has visited several (12) _____ , but so far they have no idea why
such strange things are happening.

news conference	specialists	overturns
occurrences	teenage	scary
splattered	opposite	risen
believe	faucets	reporter

STORY 14
Chain Smoker

(pages 40–42)

EXTRA PRACTICE

 First, try to write in the missing words in the blanks below. Then listen and check your work.

A (1) _____ in Missouri who wanted to (2) _____ asked his friends to "chain" him to his living room sofa for three weeks, and it (3) _____ . He hopes this is the last time he will have to (4) _____ smoking.

Forty-two-year-old Thomas Warren (5) _____ his freedom from both the chained (6) _____ and the chain-smoking late Sunday by taking a three-kilometer run, then having dinner.

Warren said that he was a very happy man, and that during the run he "felt like a bird." A (7) _____ marathon runner, he had been smoking for 20 years. He had (8) _____ to give up the habit many times before, and had tried (9) _____ , joining Smokers Anonymous, and (10) _____ , all without success.

He was smoking around a (11) _____ of cigarettes a day when he (12) _____ his friends to use a 7.5 meter steel cable to tie him to a heavy sofa.

kick the habit	former	worked
persuaded	sofa	pack
meditation	attempted	celebrated
chain smoker	quit	acupuncture

Signing Off, p. 42: Wake-up system
A The sun rises.
B The rooster crows.
C The startled hen wakes up and lays an egg.
D The egg drops into the spoon.
E The weight of the egg causes the arm to start the metronome.
F The metronome goes back and forth, pulling the string through the pulley.
G The string moves up and down, pulling on the weighted rod with the feather.
H The feather tickles the man's foot to wake him up.

STORY 15
Never Too Old

(pages 43–45)

 First, try to write in the missing words in the blanks below. Then listen and check your work.

EXTRA PRACTICE

In Los Angeles Monday, a 91-year-old American woman, Hulda Crooks, (1) _____ a plane for Japan to climb 3,776-meter Mt. Fuji, saying her (2) _____ is to get to bed early.

Ms. Crooks has climbed California's 4,412-meter Mt. Whitney 22 times and is the oldest person to climb the mountain, the highest in the (3) _____ . She was 89 when she last reached the top.

Crooks (4) _____ to spend two days climbing Mt. Fuji and has been (5) _____ for the climb. Before leaving Los Angeles on Monday, she spent 45 minutes climbing 60 steps a (6) _____ of 15 times.

Crooks began climbing mountains while in her (7) _____ after an illness, and has climbed 97 mountains since her 65th birthday. Her (8) _____ husband, a doctor, (9) _____ climbing as a way (10) _____ .

"There's too much (11) _____ among old people. I try to show them that they can still (12) _____ life."

continental United States	training	forties
to regain her strength	late	total
suggested	boarded	plans
depression	enjoy	secret

STORY 16

The Longest Wait

(pages 46–48)

EXTRA PRACTICE

 First, try to write in the missing words in the blanks below. Then listen and check your work.

After camping on the (1) _____ for 15 days, Phil Illsley bought a ballpoint pen at Selfridges (2) _____ in London Wednesday and saved 75 (3) _____ . He also set a world record for waiting the longest time for a sale.

Illsley, a 21-year-old (4) _____ from Windsor, near London, was the first of (5) _____ of shoppers allowed in for Selfridges' (6) _____ sale. After being (7) _____ by store chairman Roy Stephens, Illsley walked straight to the pen (8) _____ and bought a £2.25 Parker ballpoint pen for £1.50.

Why did he do it? "If it improves my (9) _____ , it will have been worth it."

Except for short (10) _____ , Illsley spent 360 hours just outside Selfridges' main entrance, mostly sitting and (11) _____ , and using a thermal sleeping bag for a bed.

According to the Guinness Book of (12) _____ , the previous record for the longest wait at a sale was 302 hours, 40 minutes.

handwriting	Records	thousands
pacing up and down	sidewalk	annual
department store	counter	breaks
electrician	pence	greeted

ANSWERS TO **Signing Off A,** p. 48

a. 58.4   b. 31,118

c. 57   d. 29.4

STORY 17

Romeo, Romeo

(pages 49–51)

 First, try to write in the missing words in the blanks below. Then listen and check your work.

Twenty-five-year-old Beth Corey went to the movies with her boyfriend, Kevin O'Keefe, last week and had a big (1) _____ . As they waited for the (2) _____ to begin, she saw Kevin on the (3) _____ . When she asked Kevin what was happening, he told her to keep watching.

In a short (4) _____ movie, three of O'Keefe's male friends, dressed as women, (5) _____ for his attention. But O'Keefe ignored the "women" and remained (6) _____ Corey, holding a photograph of her to his (7) _____ . He then spoke to the camera, and (8) _____ Corey.

"Beth, I love you, and I'll do (9) _____ to have you (10) _____ ... Will you marry me?" said the (11) _____ .

O'Keefe, 25, who has (12) _____ Corey for six years, had worked for a year on the four-minute film. When it was done, he asked the movie theater to play it before the main feature.

Corey said "yes."

forever	screen	competed
main feature	dated	anything
proposed to	surprise	subtitles
chest	silent	true to

Barney or Blue?

(pages 52–54)

EXTRA PRACTICE

First, try to write in the missing words in the blanks below. Then listen and check your work.

With a (1) _____ whistle in a London court yesterday, a stolen parrot

(2) _____ his owner and sent a man to jail.

Barney, an Amazon parrot (3) _____ $1,000, had been

(4) _____ from 27-year-old Georgina Morgans some months before,

and was found by police in the apartment of (5) _____

(6) _____ Eric Buckley.

In (7) _____ Buckley said the bird was his and that its name was Blue.

Ms. Morgans said the bird's name was Barney and that it was hers. So the bird was

(8) _____ into court in a covered (9) _____ and

released. When the door of the cage was opened, Barney completely

(10) _____ Buckley. Instead, he flew straight toward Ms. Morgans,

(11) _____ his own name, let out a whistle, and allowed her to

(12) _____ him under his beak.

court	recognized	suspected
stolen	ignored	worth
tickle	squawked	cage
burglar	piercing	brought